CHRISTMAS
Needlepoint Designs
Charted for Easy Use

Rita Weiss

Dover Publications Inc., New York

Published in Canada by General Publishing
Company, Ltd., 30 Lesmill Road, Don Mills,
Toronto, Ontario.
Published in the United Kingdom by Constable
and Company, Ltd., 10 Orange Street, London
WC 2.

Christmas Needlepoint Designs is a new work,
first published by Dover Publications, Inc., in
1975.

International Standard Book Number: 0-486-23161-5
Library of Congress Catalog Card Number: 74-21224

Manufactured in the United States of America
Dover Publications, Inc.
180 Varick Street
New York, N.Y. 10014

Introduction

The warm, colorful homespun quality of needlepoint makes it especially well suited to the Christmas season. Besides decorating the home with needlepoint pillows and wall hangings with Christmas motifs, the needlepointer can use needle, thread and canvas to create Christmas cards and tree ornaments as well as belts, purses, coasters and trays—all with motifs appropriate to the holiday season.

This collection consists of thirty-six designs, all graphed and ready for use on #10 needlepoint canvas. Use a single motif to make a needlepoint Christmas card, pin cushion, pocket, coaster or Christmas tree ornament. Repeat the same design or put several different ones together to make a pillow, a belt or a wall hanging. The "Twelve Days of Christmas" motifs can, of course, be done as individual pieces but they are especially effective combined as a wall hanging measuring 12½" wide by 26½" long.

Whereas these designs are shown executed in needlepoint, the graph patterns can, of course, be used in many other crafts. For cross-stitch embroidery, follow the graph by using the thread-count method on such even-weave fabrics as Aida cloth or Hardanger cloth. Knit a colored design into a basic pattern for an interesting Christmas motif on a sweater or scarf. Use one of the graphs to make a pieced-work pillow or a Christmas quilt, or even a mosaic out of tiles, seeds, sequins or beads.

Whatever the project, it is a good idea to work out a complete, detailed color scheme for the design before beginning. You will find it convenient to put tracing paper over the design in the book and to experiment with colors on the tracing paper. In this way the design in the book will not be ruined if you decide to change the colors. Suitable color combinations are suggested by the cover illustrations.

After a color scheme has been worked out, the design can be transferred to canvas. You may prefer to outline your design on the canvas itself. Since needlepoint canvas is almost transparent, it can be placed over any design in this book, and then the pattern can be traced directly onto the canvas. If you decide to paint the entire design onto the canvas make sure your medium is waterproof! Use either a nonsoluble ink, acrylic paint thinned appropriately with water so as not to clog the holes in the canvas, or oil paint mixed with benzine or turpentine. Felt-tipped pens are also very handy both for outlining and coloring in the design on the canvas, but check the labels carefully because not all felt markers are waterproof. Allow all paint to dry thoroughly before beginning the project.

The designs can also be worked directly onto the canvas by counting off the correct number of warp and woof squares shown in the diagram, each square in the grid representing one stitch to be taken on the canvas. If you have never worked a needlepoint design from a graph, you may want to begin with a simple design, such as "A Snowman," "The Herald Angel," "Silent Night, Holy Night," or "Teddy Bear in a Toy Train." These designs are, in fact, easy enough to be suitable as first projects for young children. Working a design from a graph is fun and provides an added challenge to needlepointers who have been doing all of their work on pre-painted canvases.

There are two distinct types of needlepoint canvas: single-mesh and double-mesh. Double-mesh is woven with two horizontal and two vertical threads forming each mesh, whereas single-mesh is woven with one vertical and one horizontal thread forming each mesh. Double-mesh is a very stable canvas on which the threads will stay securely in place as you work. Single-mesh canvas, which is more widely used, is a little easier on the eyes because the spaces are slightly larger.

A tapestry needle with a rounded, blunt tip and an elongated eye is used for needlepoint. The most commonly used needle for a #10 canvas is the #18 needle. The needle should clear the hole in the canvas without spreading the threads. Special yarns which have good twist and are sufficiently heavy to cover the canvas are used for needlepoint. Cloisonné, a gold metallic thread, can be used in small amounts to add sparkle to a design.

Although there are over a hundred different needlepoint stitches, these designs were all rendered in *Tent Stitch*, the stitch that is universally considered to be the needlepoint stitch. The three most familiar versions of Tent Stitch are: Plain Half-Cross Stitch, Continental Stitch and Basket Weave Stitch. The use to which you are planning to put your finished project has a great deal to do with your choice of stitch.

Plain Half-Cross Stitch, while the most economical in the use of yarn (it uses about 1 yard per square inch of canvas) is not very durable and should only be used for projects which will have little wear, such as pictures or wall hangings. It also has a tendency to pull the needlepoint out of shape, a disadvantage that can be corrected by blocking.

Continental Stitch uses slightly more yarn (about 1¼ yards per square inch), but it is more durable since the stitch works up with more thickness on the back than on the front. This is an ideal stitch for projects which will receive a great deal of wear, such as pillows, belts, purses and upholstery. The Continental Stitch also tends to pull the canvas out of shape.

The Basket Weave Stitch, which makes a very well padded and durable article, requires the same amount of yarn as the Continental Stitch, does not pull the canvas out of shape, and works up very quickly because there is no need to keep turning the canvas. It does lack maneuverability, however, and is awkward to work in areas where small shapes or intricate designs are planned. It is, however, an excellent stitch to use for large areas or backgrounds.

PLAIN HALF-CROSS STITCH: Always work Half-Cross Stitch from left to 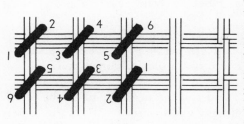 right, then turn the canvas around and work the return row, still stitching from left to right. Bring the needle to the front of the canvas at a point that will be the bottom of the first stitch. The needle is in a vertical position when making the stitch. Keep the stitches loose for minimum distortion and good coverage. This stitch must be worked on a double-mesh canvas.

CONTINENTAL STITCH: Start this design at the upper right-hand corner 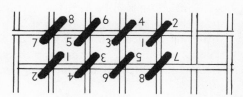 and work from right to left. The needle is slanted and always brought out a mesh ahead. The resulting stitch is actually a Half-Cross Stitch on top and a slanting stitch on the back. When the row is finished, turn the canvas around and work the return row, still stitching from right to left.

BASKET WEAVE OR DIAGONAL STITCH: Start the Basket Weave in the 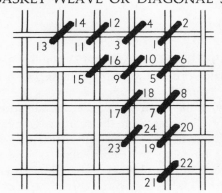 top right-hand corner (left-handed workers should begin at the lower left). Work the rows diagonally, first going down the canvas from left to right and then up the canvas from right to left. The rows must be alternated properly or a faint ridge will show where the pattern has been interrupted. Always stop working in the middle of a row rather than the end so that you will know in which direction you are working.

When starting a project, allow at least a 2″ margin of plain canvas around the needlepoint design. Bind all the raw edges of the canvas with masking tape, double-fold bias tape or even adhesive tape. There are no set rules on where to begin a design. Generally it is easier to begin close to the center and work outward toward the edges of the canvas, working the backgrounds or borders last. To avoid fraying the yarn, work with strands not longer than 18″.

When you have finished your needlepoint, it should be blocked. No matter how straight you have kept your work, blocking will give it a professional look.

Any hard, flat surface that you do not mind marring with nail holes and one that will not be warped by wet needlepoint can serve as a blocking board. A large piece of plywood, an old drawing board or an old-fashioned doily blocker are ideal.

Moisten a Turkish towel in cold water and roll the needlepoint in the towel. Leaving the needlepoint in the towel overnight will insure that both the canvas and the yarn are thoroughly and evenly dampened. Do not saturate the needlepoint! Never hold the needlepoint under the faucet as this much water is not necessary.

Mark the desired outline on the blocking board, making sure that the corners are straight. Lay the needlepoint on the blocking board, and tack the canvas with thumbtacks about ½″ to ¾″ apart. It will probably take a good deal of pulling and tugging to get the needlepoint straight, but do not be afraid of this stress. Leave the canvas on the blocking board until thoroughly dry. Never put an iron on your needlepoint. You cannot successfully block with a steam iron because the needlepoint must dry in the straightened position. You may also have needlepoint blocked professionally. If you have a pillow made, a picture framed, or a chair seat mounted, the craftsman may include the blocking in his price.

Your local needlepoint shop or department where you buy your materials will be happy to help you with any problems.

TO MAKE NEEDLEPOINT CHRISTMAS TREE ORNAMENTS: Render one motif or a section of a motif on canvas. Make a row of machine stitching around the worked area and trim the canvas ½″ from the machine stitching. Clip the corners to the machine stitching. Turn under the seam allowance and slipstitch in place. Cut a piece of felt approximately 1″ larger than the trimmed canvas. Slipstitch the needlepoint to the felt backing, trimming the felt to the appropriate shape as you work. Since felt has a tendency to stretch out of shape as it is being worked, it is a good idea to work in this manner rather than to cut the felt to the exact shape in the beginning. Double a piece of thread, approximately 8″ to 10″ long (gold Cloisonné is ideal) and attach to the back of the ornament as a loop. You can make round or triangular ornaments by working backgrounds in these shapes. A completed tree ornament made from a section of the "Choir of Angels" motif appears on the front cover.

TO MAKE NEEDLEPOINT CHRISTMAS CARDS: Render one motif on canvas, filling in enough background so that the completed needlepoint will measure 3½" x 5" (35 by 50 meshes). Block to size. Cut a strip of cardboard or heavy paper 6½" x 15". Mark lengthwise into three sections, each 5" x 6½", and make an accordion fold. From the top third, cut a rectangle 3½" x 5", leaving a ¾" frame all around. Center the blocked needlepoint in the frame and staple or tape in place, using the middle section of the card as a backing. Write your Christmas message on the bottom third of the card. The recipient can use the finished needlepoint for a pin cushion, patch, or even as a miniature Christmas wall hanging. Two completed Christmas cards made from "A Christmas Lantern" and "Poinsettias" appear on the front cover of this book.

TO MAKE A NEEDLEPOINT CHRISTMAS BELT: Use one of the horizontal designs, repeating the pattern and using enough background so that the completed belt will be 3½" wide and the desired length. Trim the canvas, leaving a ½" seam allowance all around. Cut a piece of lining material of suitable color the same size as the trimmed canvas. Turn under the seam allowances on both canvas and lining, and whip the lining to the needlepoint, wrong sides facing. Sew hooks and eyes or buckle in place.

TO MAKE NEEDLEPOINT PIN CUSHIONS: Render one motif 3½" x 5" and block. Make a row of machine stitching around the worked area to prevent raveling and trim the canvas ½" from the machine stitching. Turn under ½" on all sides and slipstitch in place. Cut a 4½" x 6" piece of backing out of velvet, velveteen or corduroy and baste under ½" on all edges of the backing. Hand stitch the backing to the front with even stitches, leaving an opening to stuff. Stuff firmly and then stitch over the opening.

TO MAKE NEEDLEPOINT CHRISTMAS PILLOWS: Since standard pillow forms come in 12", 14", 16" and 18" squares, use enough motifs (repeating the same design or using two or three different designs in a patchwork pattern) and/or add borders to fill the required area. Block to the required size. Trim the canvas, leaving a ½" seam allowance on all sides. Cut a backing of the same size as the canvas out of velvet, velveteen, corduroy or similar fabric in a color that matches the main color in the needlepoint. With right sides together machine stitch the needlepoint to the backing. Turn right side out and insert the pillow form. Whip stitch the open edges. You might also find it fun to work some of the designs with rug yarn on #5 canvas for pillows. The pillow on the front cover is "Santa Claus Smoking His Pipe" worked on a #5 canvas. Using this larger mesh canvas makes the pillow quick and easy to complete.

TO MAKE THE "TWELVE DAYS OF CHRISTMAS" WALL HANGING (see illustration): The finished wall hanging will measure 12½″ wide by 26½″ long. To allow for a 2″ margin of plain canvas all around, begin with a piece of canvas that is 16½″ x 30½″. The needlepoint is worked on 125 meshes across and 265 meshes down. The Christmas motifs are worked three across and four deep, with a ½″ frame (5 meshes) at the top and bottom, at each side and between each design. Choose a contrasting color for this frame. The title is worked in 2 sections of 15 rows each, one near the top and the other near the bottom of the hanging.

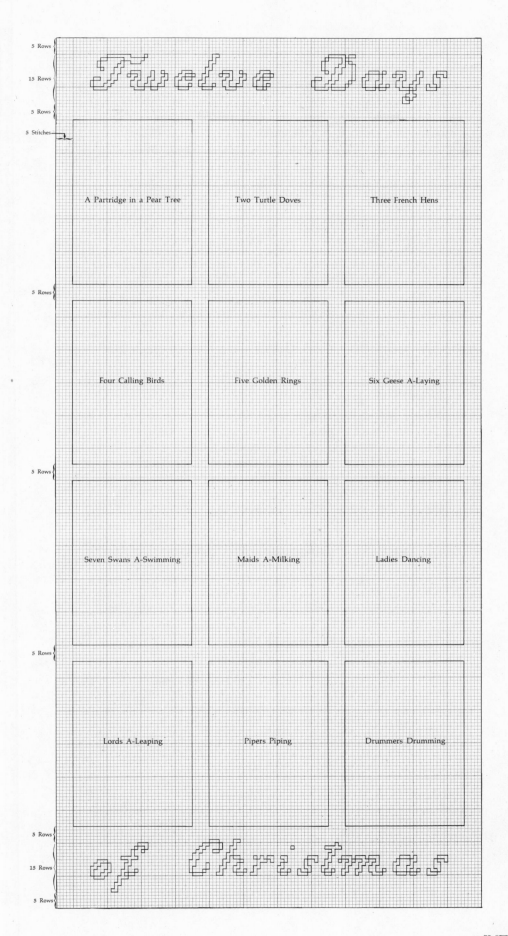

5 Rows

15 Rows

5 Rows

5 Stitches

A Partridge in a Pear Tree   Two Turtle Doves   Three French Hens

5 Rows

Four Calling Birds   Five Golden Rings   Six Geese A-Laying

5 Rows

Seven Swans A-Swimming   Maids A-Milking   Ladies Dancing

5 Rows

Lords A-Leaping   Pipers Piping   Drummers Drumming

5 Rows

15 Rows

5 Rows

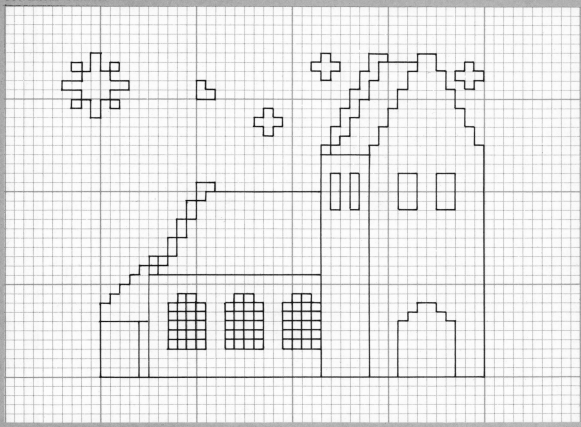

Silent Night, Holy Night

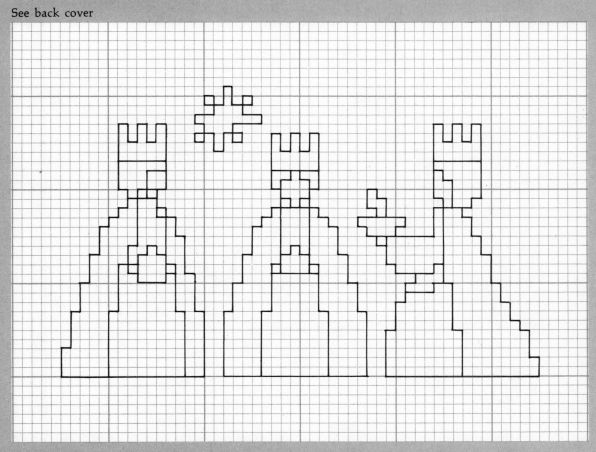

The Three Kings

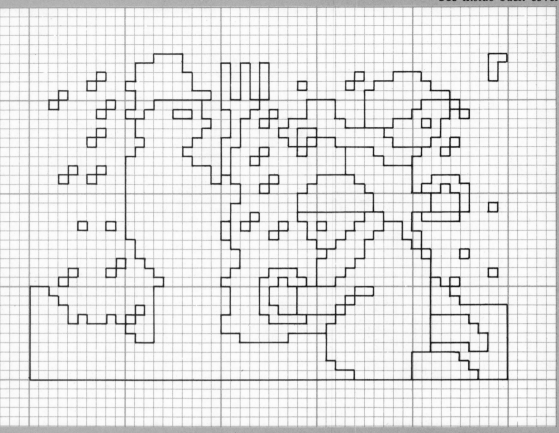

Building a Snowman

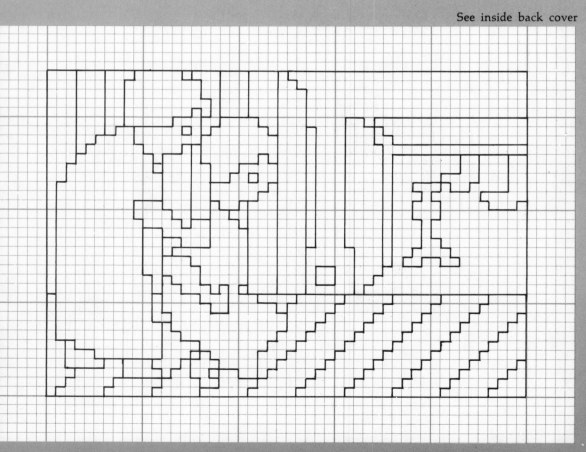

Waiting for Santa Claus

See inside back cover

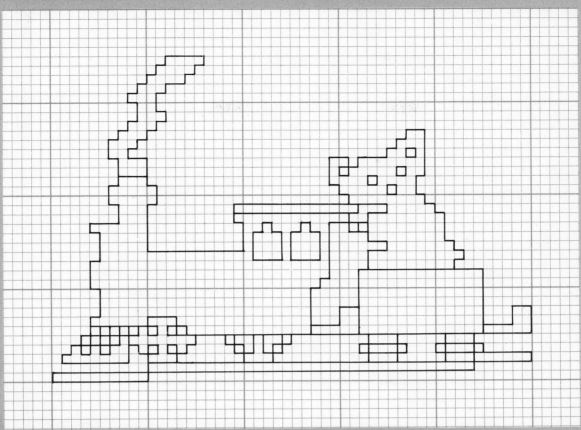

Teddy Bear in a Toy Train

See back cover

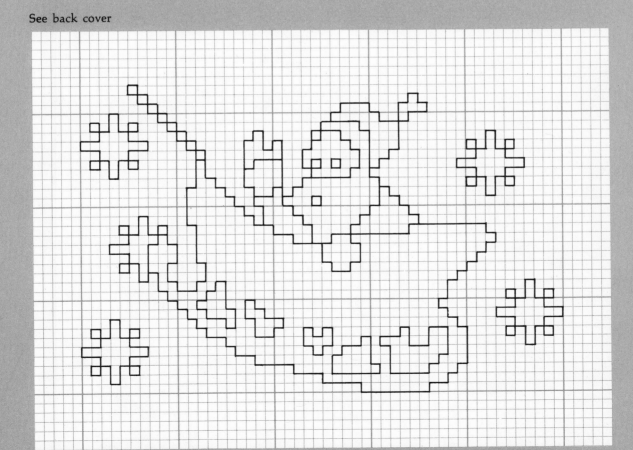

Santa Claus in His Sled

See back cover

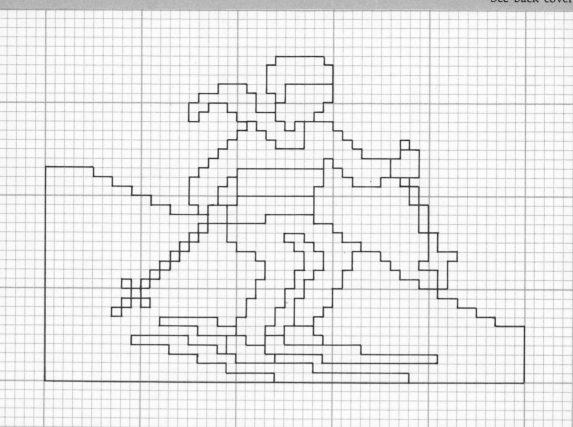

The Skier

See inside back cover

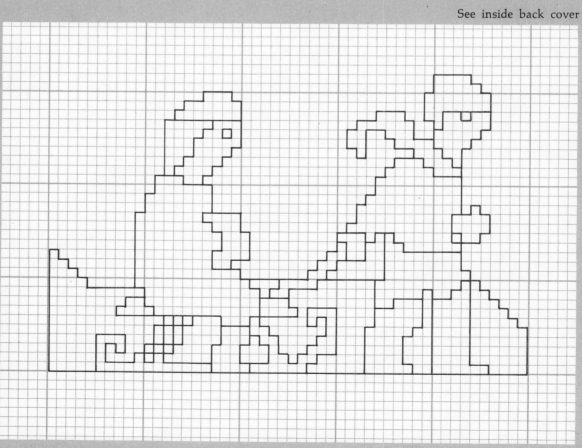

Children Playing with a Sled

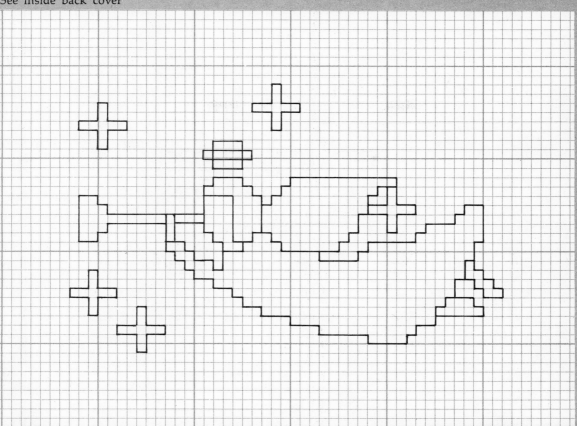

The Herald Angel

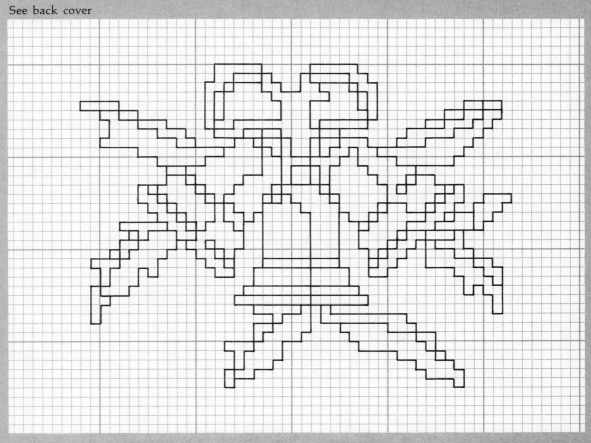

Christmas Bells

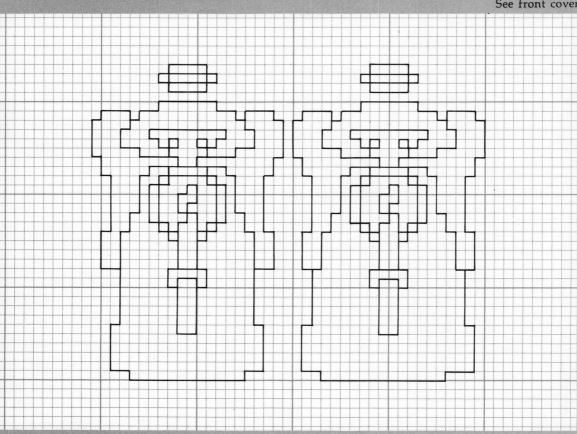

Choir of Angels

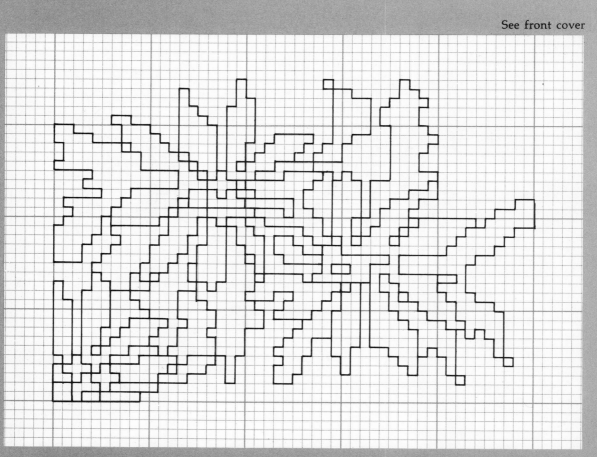

Poinsettias

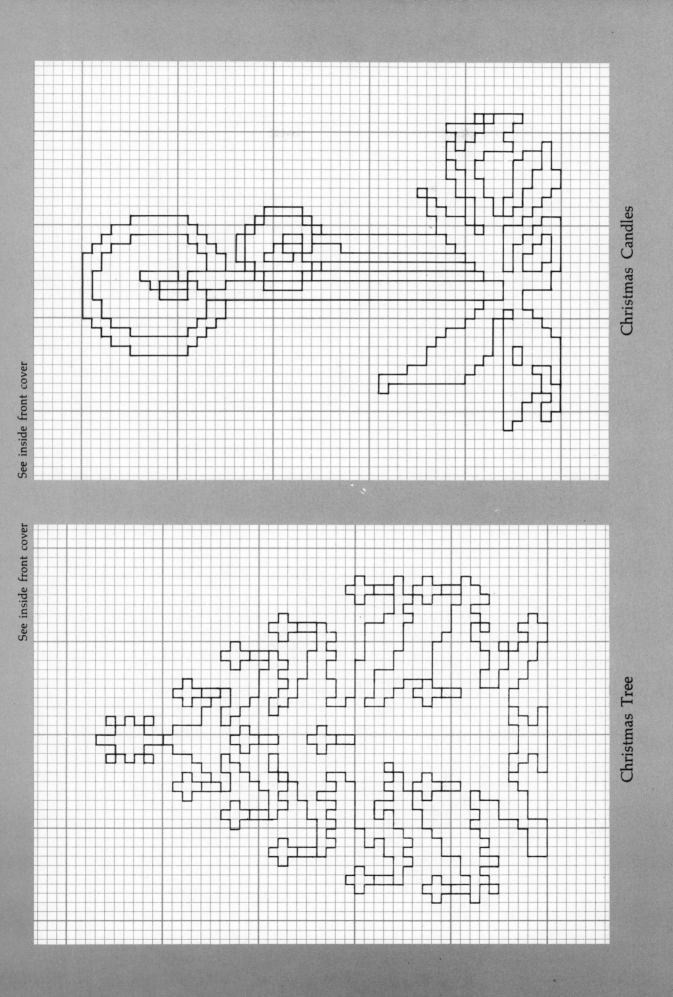

See inside front cover

Christmas Candles

See inside front cover

Christmas Tree

7

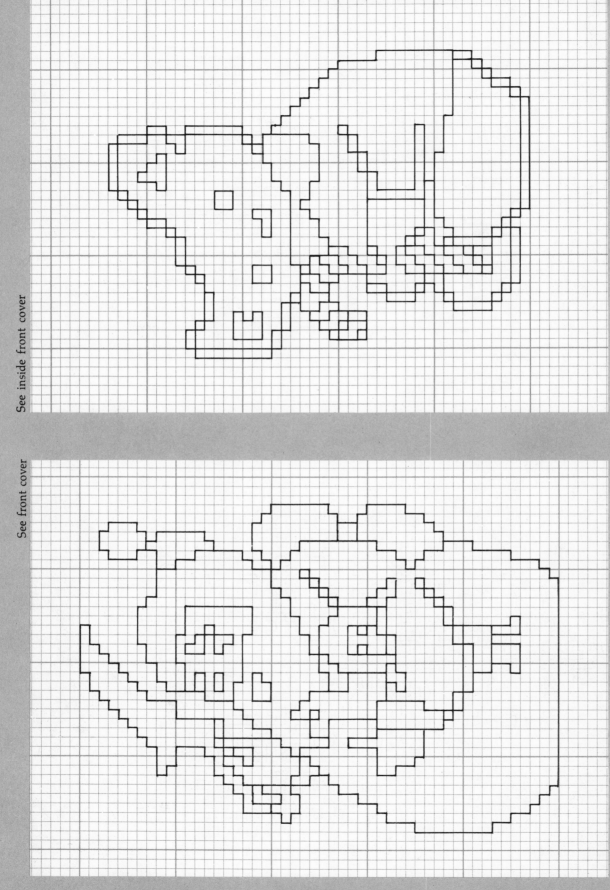

See inside front cover

Teddy Bear with a Candy Cane

See front cover

Santa Claus Smoking His Pipe (apologies to Thomas Nast)

8

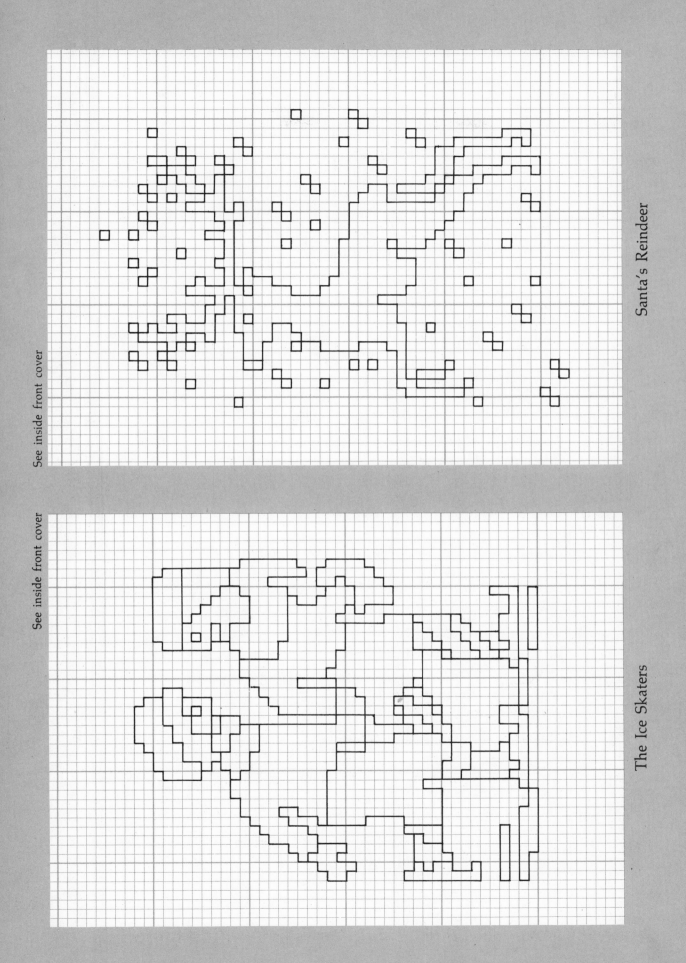

Santa's Reindeer

The Ice Skaters

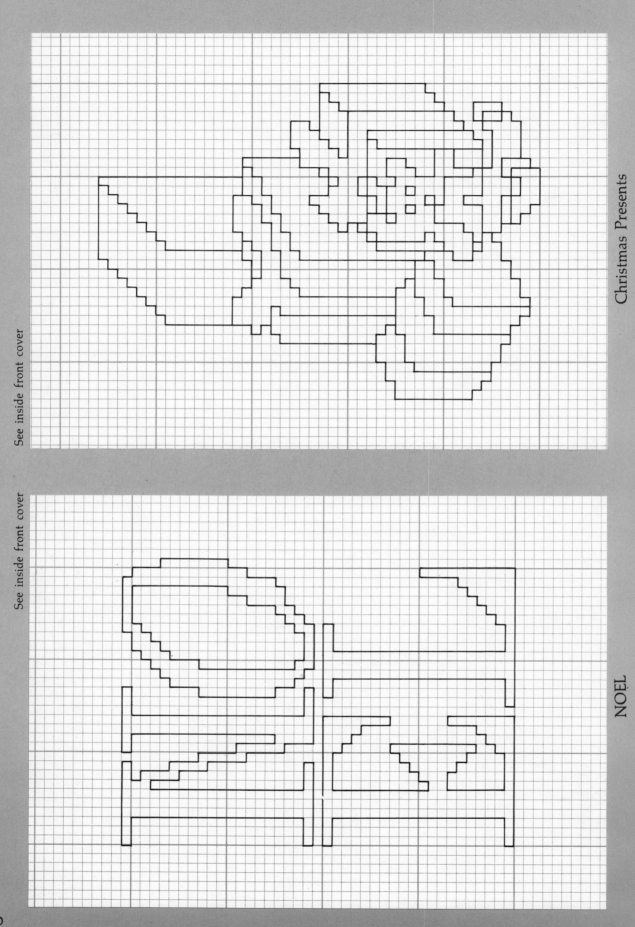

See inside front cover

See inside front cover

Christmas Presents

NOËL

10

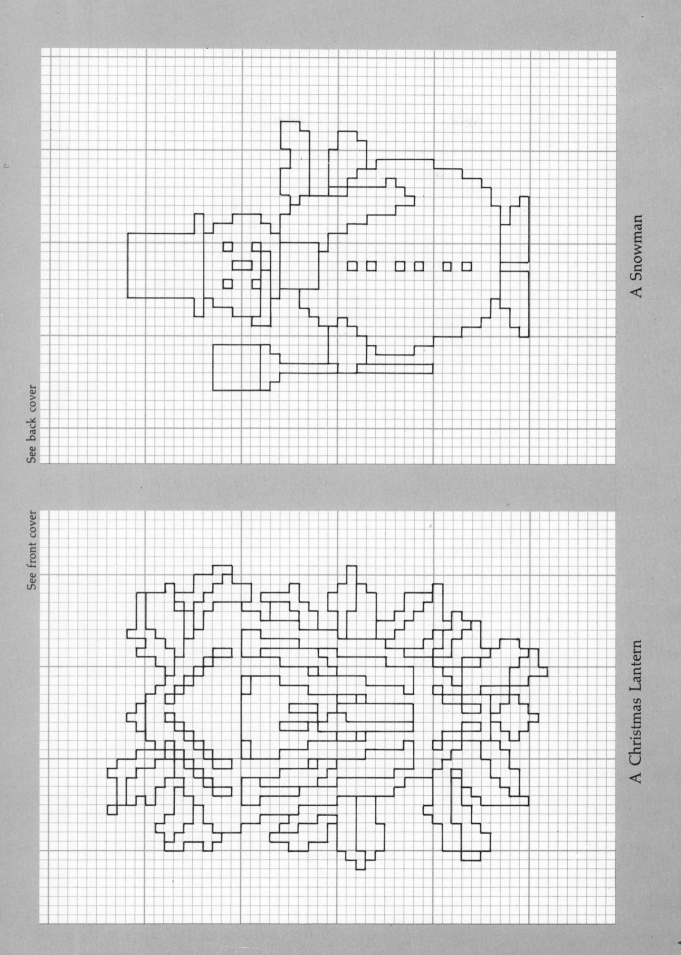

See back cover

A Snowman

See front cover

A Christmas Lantern

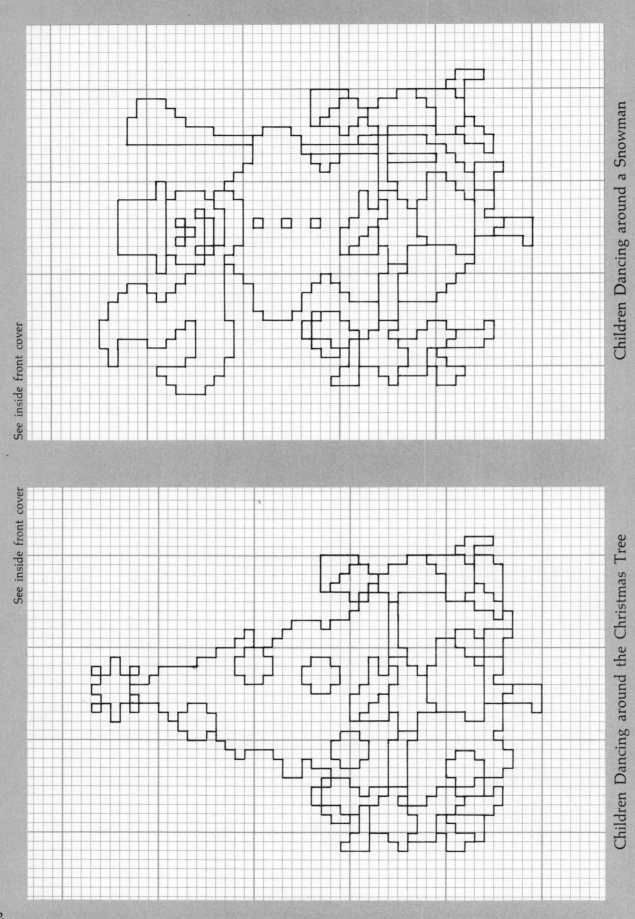

Children Dancing around a Snowman

Children Dancing around the Christmas Tree

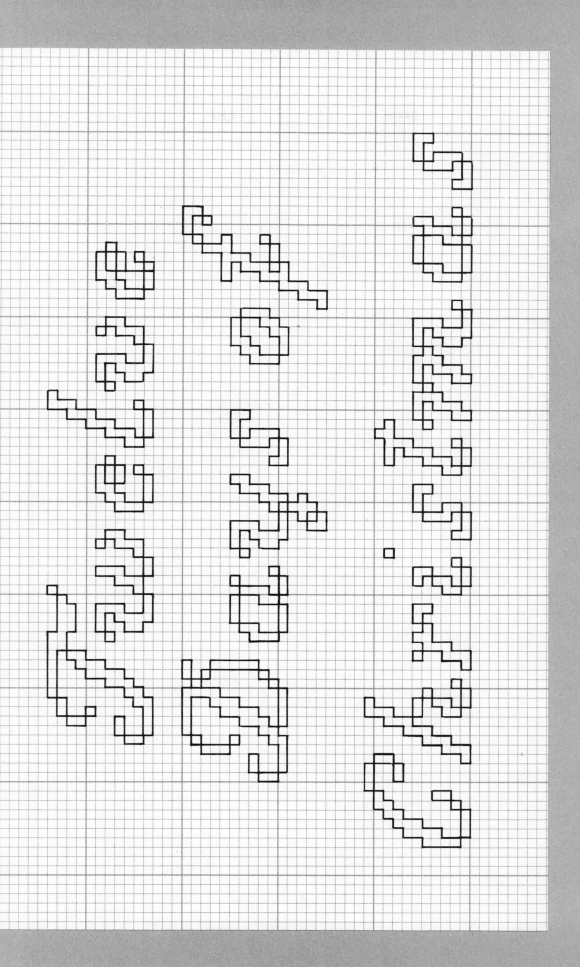

13

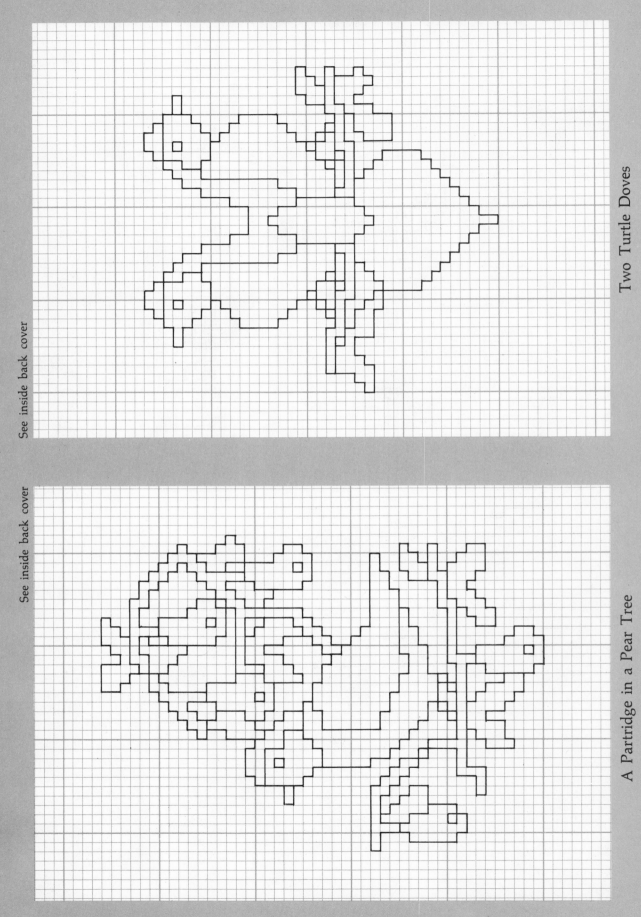

See inside back cover

Two Turtle Doves

See inside back cover

A Partridge in a Pear Tree

14

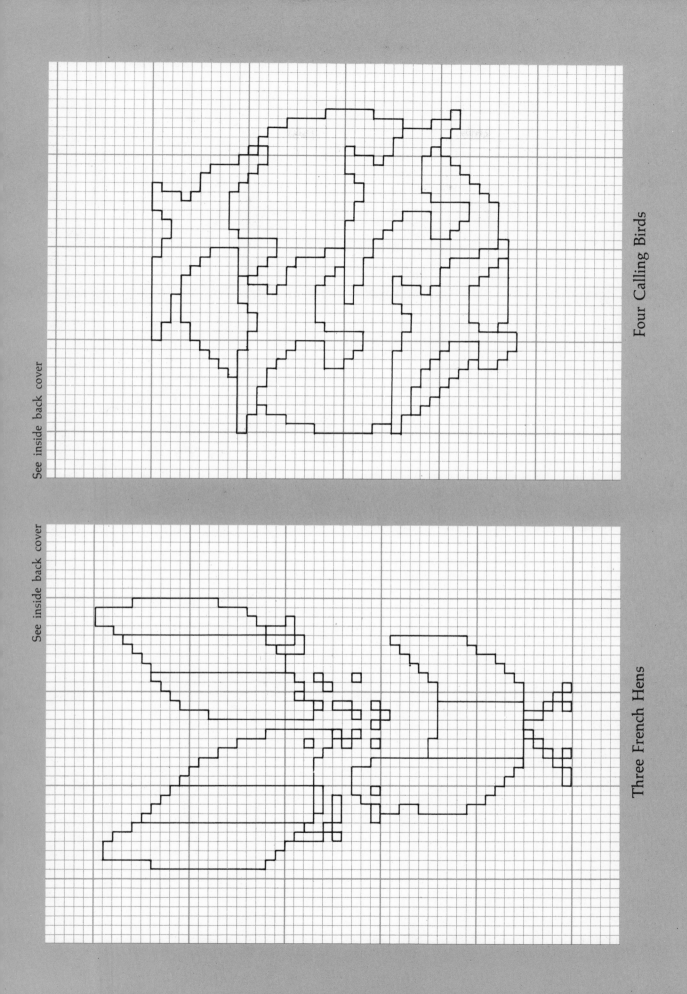

See inside back cover

Four Calling Birds

See inside back cover

Three French Hens

See inside back cover

Six Geese A-Laying

See inside back cover

Five Golden Rings

16

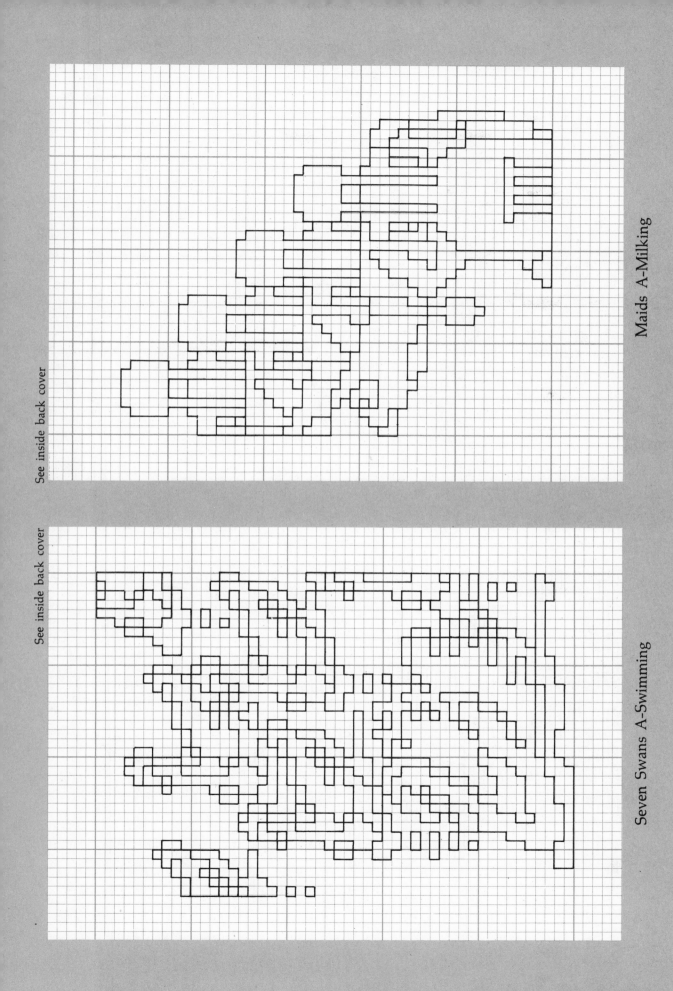

See inside back cover

Maids A-Milking

See inside back cover

Seven Swans A-Swimming

17

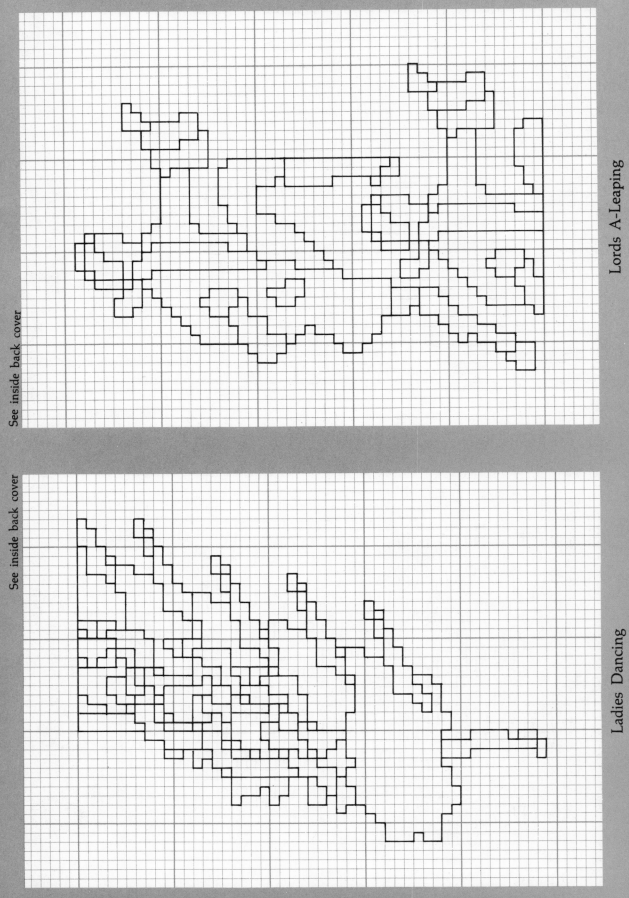

See inside back cover

Lords A-Leaping

See inside back cover

Ladies Dancing

Drummers Drumming

Pipers Piping

19